How To Buy Gold For Profit Without Money or Experience

Preface

Choosing a cover and title of a book is arguably one of the hardest, but most important decisions to make. Unless you are a famous author, the cover is likely the only asset of your book that your potential readers will see. If your cover doesn't succeed in telling your books story, you are more than likely doomed.

I originally had a cover done for this book by a professional with a photo they used from either a picture they took, or photo that they bought from an online database. After reviewing the cover, I decided it didn't succeed in capturing the content inside this book. After some thought, I made the decision to take a photo of some of the gold jewelry that I have purchased using the methods explained in this book. I wanted to provide you with physical evidence that these strategies work even before you have opened the first page of this book.

After piling up some of the gold for the photo, I paused and reflected on how each jewelry piece had a story and a person behind it. I am very grateful that I chose to shoot my own cover, as I probably would have never took the time to appreciate the beauty of meeting new people, and purchasing astonishing items for such a great price. I am very thankful for all the nice people, places, and opportunities that gold buying has brought to me, and the cover of this book is a reflection of some of those stories.

Table of Contents

Introduction

In this short book, I am going to teach you a step by step process on how to buy gold jewelry and sell it for a profit. I have been doing this for over 8 years, and have developed a strategy that you can use to make a couple hundred extra dollars a month, to a few thousand dollars a month depending on how dedicated you are to finding the deals.

In this book, I will go over the following:

- **The top 5 reasons to become a gold buyer**
- **How to Buy Gold With a Zero Interest Credit Card**
- **How to Use Other People's Money to**

Buy Gold

- **How to Approach Investors For Financing**
- **How to Value Gold**
- **How to Test Gold**
- **Where to Buy Gold**
- **How to Sell Gold**

Avoiding Mistakes

Although making mistakes are often inevitable, the steps in this book are designed to help you avoid making the big mistakes. I have made every mistake I can probably think of, and I want to save you time and money by helping you avoid them.

Once you finish this book, you will have the knowledge you will need to become a gold buyer. You will literally be able to start making money within a week from reading this. You may even be able to quit your job by using these strategies. The deals are all around you, it is up to you if you want to find them.

Top 5 Reasons to Become a Gold Buyer

Reason 1: Gold Has Tremendous Value

Gold is extremely valuable, and you can fit a tremendous amount of wealth in a very small amount of space. This will allow you to be able to purchase thousands of dollars of gold, and literally fit your business in a tiny box.

One of the biggest setbacks of owning any kind of business is that you need room for your inventory, and storing and transporting inventory can be very costly. This is why becoming a gold buyer is an opportunity for everyone. Whether you live in a studio apartment, or a mansion, it really makes no difference. Space is not a constraint in this business, and having the money really isn't a problem to get started either.

Reason 2: Gold Is Extremely Liquid

Gold is one of the most liquid assets on this planet. You can carry an ounce of gold in your pocket and it is worth the same amount of money, to everyone, everywhere, at the same time. Unlike buying and selling other goods and services, you don't need to waste your time to find the right buyer at the right price when you sell because we are all selling gold based on the current spot price.

You can find a buyer of your gold within 5 minutes, and that buyer will pay the same price for your gold as a buyer 1,000 miles away from you.

Reason 3: Gold is in a Bull Market

I believe we are in a secular bull market in gold, but are close to completing a cyclical bear market within the secular bull market. For those that are confused with this terminology let me clarify. Basically, gold has been in an uptrend since the year 2001 starting at about $250 per ounce and it got all the way up to around $1,900 per ounce in August of 2011 where it peaked in price (secular bull market). Since 2011, gold has been falling in price for over 3 years now (cyclical bear market), but is near its long term up trend line that was started in the early part of the year 2001.

Gold has stabilized over the last year, and I believe the uptrend will remain intact causing gold to increase in price gradually over time. I believe this to be true whether you live in the United States, or outside the U.S. because with most major countries the gold price is in a long term uptrend in their respected currencies. A gradual rise in price will help the deals you find become more valuable as time goes on.

Reason 4: You Can Find Great Deals

Buying gold outside of the stock exchange, or outside of gold dealers gives you an advantage. The reason being you can buy it below the current spot price of gold which immediately guarantees you a profit. If you purchase a coin from a dealer, or buy it on the stock exchange, you have to pay a premium above spot for a coin, and you have to pay a brokerage fee for a trade on the stock exchange.

There is nothing wrong with using these vehicles for purchasing gold, however, you start off with a small loss and lose your leverage. Searching for the deals allows you to increase your profits and minimize risk. The goal for you is to become a virtual gold miner without the headaches of mining for gold in the traditional sense.

Reason 5: It Is Easy To Get Started

To become a gold buyer, you really only need about $30 to start, and you can find most of the deals by sitting on your computer, smart phone, or tablet.

Below is an itemized list and cost of what you need to start:

Digital Jewelry Scale: $8

Rare Earth Magnet: $8
Jewelers Loupe: $4
Acid Testing Kit: $10
Calculator: Free (On Smart Phone)

Total Cost = $30

It may cost a little more if you prefer to purchase more expensive equipment, but $30 is all you truly need to get started. You will also want to store your equipment in a nice box or brief case.

How much easier can this be? You can buy gold for profit using your computer at home, with little space, and you can start with as little as $30.

It really is that simple if you follow our guidelines outlined in this book you are almost guaranteed to make money. However, this book is not a get rich quick scheme. You do need to put hard work and effort into making this dream become your profitable reality.

Gold's Bear Market Has Wiped Out The Competition.

The last 3 years in particular have been tough to be a gold buyer. I have seen many gold buying shops giving up and throwing closed signs on their door along with all the "We Buy Gold" TV ads vanishing. Personally, I think there is light at the end of the tunnel. While the amateurs will still be feeling the pain from the previous price correction in the gold market, the baton will be passed on to the newcomers with a fresh start. If I am correct, and we are near a low in the gold price, this will give you an opportunity to gain ground before the majority realizes that the bull market is back.

Gold's Bull Market

Below is a price chart of gold in all major currencies.

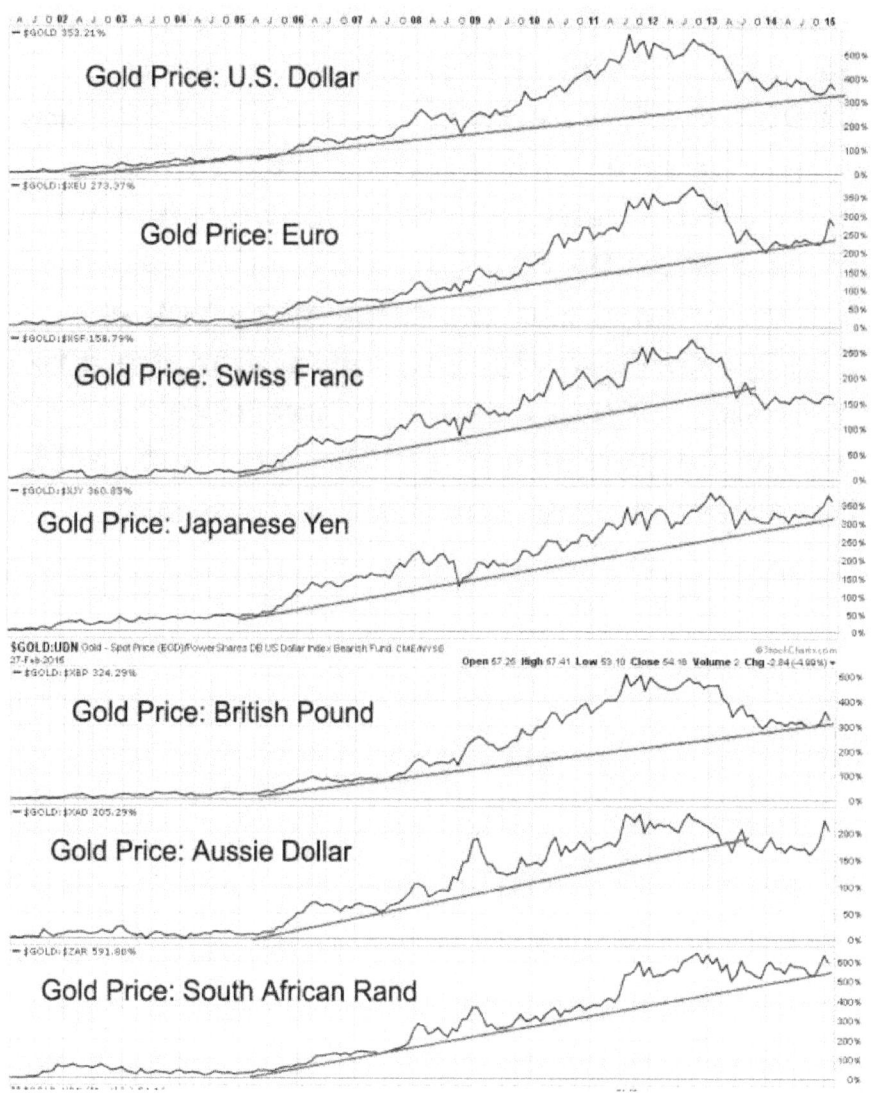

Gold has been in an uptrend in all currencies since about 2001.

Shown on the next page is the start of the gold bull market. As you can see it started in the year 2001 below $300 per ounce and has gradually made it all the way up to $1,900. As I write this, we are at $1,200 per ounce and near long term support of the trend line. I believe it will most likely hold around $1,100 - $1,200, and resume upward. If I am wrong, and the price goes below $1,100, don't worry, you can still make a ton of money buying gold. You just have to follow our guidelines strictly, and become the smart money, not the dumb money.

Purchasing Gold With Credit

Now you might be thinking that you want to start buying gold, but you have no money to start out. That is perfectly ok. If you have decent credit, and not a ton of credit card debt, you most likely receive weekly credit card offers in the mail. More often than not, these credit card offers have a 0% APR introductory rate for 15 months on them. The nice thing about these offers is that you are literally printing your own money, and you can use these card offers to get started right away!

Risk / Reward

It is important to note that there is some risk involved by doing this. The risks are very straight forward and common sense. If you don't make a profit on your purchases by the time your zero interest runs out, you will have to find additional money to pay it off. If you don't make the minimum monthly payments, or you fail to pay off the entire balance of the credit card prior to the 0% interest offer, you can be subject to additional interest rate fees. These fees can often be extremely high, and be a financial setback. If you have had trouble making payments on bills or credit cards in the past, and lack financial education, I would recommend that you skip buying gold with credit and save enough money to get started as soon as you can. If you have financial discipline, this is a great way to get started in the gold business.

The only place you are going to be able purchase gold with a zero interest credit card are at the estate sales and auctions. Most estate sales, and online auctions accept credit cards, but prior to attending an estate sale, you can check to see if they accept credit cards. Once you start purchasing gold on your credit card, you then have the ability to sell it to turn it back into cash which will then allow you to purchase gold with cash at places that won't accept credit cards.

If you are looking to only purchase gold on

Craigslist there is a trick you can use to extract cash from your zero interest credit card without the fees. This again takes financial discipline and is not for everyone. The fastest way to extract cash from your credit card is to designate your expenses to your zero interest credit card that you normally would pay with your own savings. Start charging only your necessities to your credit card and then start using your extra cash to purchase gold from the additional money you have saved from diverting your expenses to the 0% credit card. The biggest temptation you will have is to buy crap you don't need which will defeat the purpose of this method. If you don't have financial discipline, this method is not for you.

Using Other People's Money

If you don't like the credit card idea, or don't receive the 0% credit card offers, you may want to try and approach a friend or someone that you know that has a little bit of money.

Interest rates are extremely low, and will likely be low for as far as the eye can see. Savers are losers in this environment, and there are some very frustrated savers out there that don't know what to do.

Offer your potential investor a solution to their problem. Offer them an interest rate for a short term loan above what their bank will give them. Explain what you are going to use it for which will strictly be to buy gold so that they have an asset behind their savings that is extremely liquid, and can be turned back into cash at any given time.

If you are going to utilize this approach, make sure you are financially disciplined, and will only use their money to purchase gold. Write a contract with all the specific details of your loan so that you both can sign, and are all on the same page. I cannot stress enough that using credit or leverage can increase your risks of loss.

Why not just ask a bank for a loan to buy gold?

You can ask your bank for a personal loan,

but the problem is it will be at a pretty high interest rate. Even though interest rates are extremely low, personal loans are running above 5%-7% depending on your credit.

The reason why personal loans are so high is because there isn't an asset behind the loan that the bank can legally acquire if they loan you the money and you fail to make payments.

You are of course purchasing gold with their money, but the legal terms on a personal loan does not distinguish between a person using loaned money for a vacation to the person using their loan money to buy gold.

For these reasons, it is easier to seek out frustrated savers over going to a bank. You will get a lower interest rate than the bank will give you, and your investor will get a higher rate on their savings. It is a win win situation.

Now that you have your money source in mind, let's get into the steps of gold buying...

How to Weigh and Value Gold

The first thing that you need to do to get started with buying gold is purchase the tools listed in the beginning of this book. These tools include a strong rare earth magnet, digital jewelry scale, jewelers loupe, gold acid testing kit, and a calculator if you don't have one on your phone. You can order this entire list at one time on Amazon and most likely receive free shipping. Once you receive your items in the mail you can follow the steps to weigh any gold item, and determine the value.

Step 1:

Run your magnet over your item. No part should be attracted to the magnet EXCEPT if you have a clasp. The clasp is most often going to attract the magnet because it needs to be a sturdier material than gold, and the spring inside the clasp is not gold. The picture below shows what it looks like when your gold item is plated and has filler material that attracts the magnet. If the magnet attracts it is not solid gold.

Step 2:

Make sure the unit is on grams. To make sure your scale is accurate, place a penny on top of the scale to make sure it weighs 2.5 grams. If it weighs in correctly, you can now weigh your item. If it does not weigh correctly, follow the instructions provided with your scale to re calibrate your scale.

If your item is larger than the scale, you can use the cover as a tray to expand the scale size. To do this you first turn on the scale, and then place the tray on the scale which will then show the weight of the tray. You then hit the "zero" button and it should appear as "0" weight on the display to cancel out the weight of the tray on the scale. Your item is now ready to be weighed.

 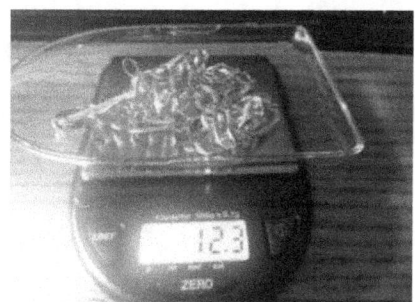

Step 3:

After you finish weighing your item, you then need to find out the karat of your item which can usually be found by the stamp on the jewelry. It is either going to be stamped 10k, 14k, 18k, and sometimes 22k. Gold jewelry from the Middle East, India, and some parts of Asia are usually 22k. Most often you can read these stamps without a magnifying glass or jewelers loupe, but it would probably be a good idea to always have one on you to make sure you can read every stamp.

You might often see a decimal number on the stamp instead of the traditional karat markings. This represents the percentage of gold in the piece and is generally an authentic stamp of real gold.

The following stamped numbers are for each gold type.

10k - 417
14k - 585
18k - 750
22k - 917

Keep an eye out for gold filled or gold plated items. You do not want to purchase any of these items even if they are offering you a cheap price. Stick with solid gold.

Examples of Stamps That Are Not Solid Gold:

14k 1/20 - Plated or Gold Filled
14k G.F. - Gold Filled
14k G.P. - Gold Plated

14k H.G.E - Hydrostatic Gold Electroplated
14k G.E.P. - Gold Electroplated

Once you determine the karat of your item, you are ready to calculate your items value.

Steps for calculating the gold price in grams

Step 1

The first thing you will need to do is find the current market value of gold which can be found at www.goldseek.com keep in mind that the gold price changes every minute of the day Monday – Friday.

Once you look up the gold price, take the price per ounce divided by 31.1 which is how many grams are in an ounce. This allows you to know how much the gold price is per gram of pure 24k gold.

For example, if gold was trading at $1,270 per oz and you divided it by 31.1 – you get $40.83 per gram of pure gold.

Step 2

To find out what purity each karat has of gold you take the karat number divided by 24.

For example 14k gold would be. 14 /24 = .583

The percentages are as follows:

22k gold = .91 percent
18k gold = .75 percent
14k gold = .58 percent
10k gold = .41 percent

Step 3

Find out the price per gram for each karat by multiplying the current gram price of pure gold by the percentages above. In the example above, we are multiplying $40.83 per gram times each karat.

The price per gram for gold trading at $1,271 per ounce $40.83 per gram would be as follows:

24k gold = $40.83 per gram
22k gold = $37.15 per gram
18k gold = $30.62 per gram
14k gold = $23.68 per gram
10k gold= $16.74 per gram

Diamonds

When buying gold, it will be inevitable that you are going to come across some diamonds. Most of the stuff I buy that has diamonds in it are very small, and are not worth much. Occasionally you may be asked to remove the diamond, or sometimes people just don't care about the smaller diamonds and it is yours to keep. Most woman's gold rings at today's gold prices are only worth about $50 so it is up to you to decide if it would be worth your time removing a diamond or not. You can remove diamonds relatively easy by using a fine wire snips to cut the prongs holding the diamonds in place. However, the tiny diamonds are sometimes extremely difficult to remove without damaging the diamond itself.

Selling the diamonds you accumulate is a way different process than selling gold. There is only one gold price to go by, and you will find that anyone in the industry will pay same price at or around the spot price.

Although diamond prices have sky rocketed in the past few years, each one is priced by a ton of different factors, and each diamond requires the right buyer.

The easiest way to sell diamonds is establishing a relationship with a jewelry store that has a good reputation. They should be able to give you a fair price for your diamonds. What I personally do is just hold on to them. I figure if I didn't pay for them in the first place, there is nothing wrong with accumulating a personal stash of diamonds.

How to Test Gold

The final step is to make sure your gold is authentic. This can be tricky. Most gold content is what it says on the stamp. However, it is always a good idea to double check to make sure you are buying real gold. When I first started out, I just went by the stamp which worked fine on 99% of the items, but as soon as I found out one of the items that I purchased wasn't real gold, I immediately started to test the gold to make sure it was authentic.

Acid Testing

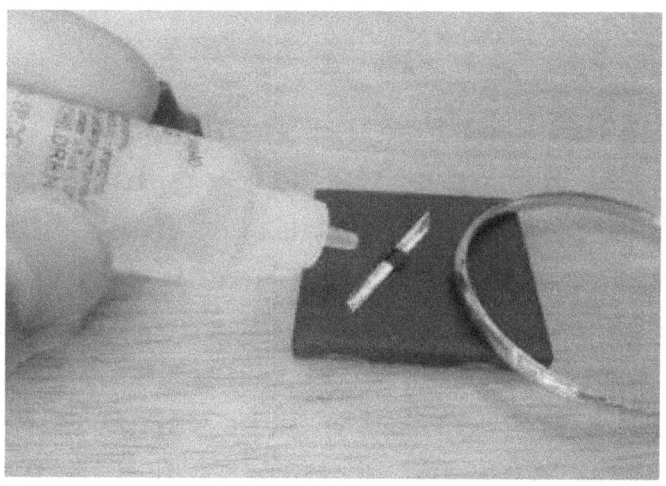

You can purchase a gold acid test kit for about $10 on Amazon. This is by far the cheapest way to test gold, but it is not my favorite. The reason is that you have to sand the gold down before you buy it, and have to deal with chemicals. Even though it is not my favorite way, it is very effective in helping you determine the karat of you gold.

Steps for testing gold with acid

Step 1:

Rub your gold item on the provided scratch pad so that a line of gold shavings can be seen on the pad.

Step 2:

Look at the karat of the stamp on your item, and place a drop of the same gold karat solution, and observe the reaction. If the solution remains clear, and you can still see the gold shavings, then you can move on to the next form of acid that is higher. After you move to the next higher karat acid, you then place another drop on your shavings. If the shavings completely disappear, you know the karat is the karat lower from your last test that dissolved the metal.

For example, if you are testing 14k gold, start with 14k acid, and if there is no reaction to that acid, you then place an 18k acid drop on your shavings. If the 18k acid makes the gold shavings disappear, then you know the gold you are testing is the karat below the acid that dissolved the shavings which would be 14k.

Electronic Testing

After you have started to purchase gold for a while, and start making money, I would suggest purchasing an electronic tester with some of your proceeds. You can purchase a variety of electronic gold testers which range from $100 - $300. The reason why these are nice is you are not using acid and they are accurate. They work by running electricity through your item which determines the karat by the electric current flowing in your item.

I prefer the GemOro Auracle AGT2 electronic gold tester. You can conveniently test your gold with a kit that hooks up to your phone and you can log each item you test. It is a personal favorite of mine, and is very convenient.

Specific Gravity

Another way to test your gold is by doing a specific gravity test. There are machines for this that calculates the specific gravity of your item for you, but the setback is they cost over $1,800. I own one of these machines, and it is helpful. However, there are setbacks that relying solely on specific gravity testing is not a good idea. If there are any bubbles around your item in water it will give you an inaccurate reading, and it is difficult to get rid of the bubbles on certain items.

There is also a very inexpensive way to measure the specific gravity of your item. All you need is your scale, a glass of water, and a way to submerge your item inside the glass of water with a string without touching the edges of the glass.

X-ray Machine

Another way to test gold is an X-ray gun. These guns are about $20,000 to purchase, and they give an extremely accurate reading what exactly is inside your item. There is no reason for you to purchase one of these, however, some metal recycling places will have them, and they often will assess your items for free or at a small charge.

If you are in question, it is well worth a few bucks to find out! A few times I have come across gold shavings or dental gold that I was having a very hard time using the traditional methods so I brought it to the recycling place to have it x-rayed. One of the items I almost purchased looked like gold, but it ended up being 96% aluminum. I almost purchased those aluminum shavings for $2,000 because I thought it was gold! The shavings were not worth more than 10 cents!

Where to Buy Gold

Any gold that you can get 15-20% below the spot price is an immediate potential profit for you. Never buy gold above the spot price unless you really want to keep the piece for your personal use. The reason is because if you purchase an item over spot, you cannot guarantee you will be able to sell it in a short amount of time. It can take days or months to find the right buyer of gold that you purchase over spot, and could lead to potential losses.

Friends and Family

When I first started purchasing gold jewelry, I started with buying jewelry from friends and family. I just asked them if they had any old gold they wanted to get rid of. To my surprise, almost everyone I asked had over $200 worth of gold that was just sitting in a box collecting dust. The first purchase I made was my dad's class ring. I gave him $250 for it, and he ended up buying a grill with the proceeds. Soon after him telling people he bought his grill with his class ring, other family members and friends started approaching me to buy their gold, and it took off from there. The nice thing about practicing with your family is that you can take your time to calculate the value and you don't feel under pressure like you would in other situations. So once you practice on your family, you can move on to find deals in other avenues.

Craigslist

There are books written on gold buying that claim it is easy to buy gold by creating your own "I Will Buy Your Gold" ad on Craiglist. I found this to be a hit and miss strategy. You will find that often users will report your ad as spam on the jewelry page which terminates your ad immediately, and you will have to keep re-posting your ad each time it gets taken down. The other thing I have found about these ads is for the most part, the majority of the people that contact you are asking a price way above what you are going to be looking for, and they will also call you about stuff you just won't want to buy. You often end up meeting people for no reason and wasting your time and money. I would recommend trying to post your own ads a few times to see how it goes, but it is not a strategy that you should solely rely on.

The nice thing about browsing CL is that they have a photo, a description, and a price that you can quickly click through to see if it meets your criteria. If it meets your buying criteria, you can contact them, if it doesn't you just move on to the next item.

90% of CL is full of overpriced jewelry. However, if you are patient, you can always find deals on CL. Just simply search in the areas you are willing to travel to and weed out the bad deals, and keep track of the good ones.

Using Filters To Make Your Searches Efficient:

Step 1

Go to craiglist and on the right side click "cities." All the major cities will pop up on the right in alphabetical order.

Step 2
Click on the City that is most relevant to your area.

Step 3
Select the Jewelry section.

Step 4
On the left side of the page select "by owner." then select the two boxes "search titles only" and "has image."

Step 5
On the top of the page there are buttons selection that say "list, thumb, gallery, map" Select "thumb" for thumbnail.

Step 4 and 5 are to narrow down your searches and allow you to easily browse through items without having to click on every one of them.

How to Search on Craig's List

Next you will use search terms to find specific pieces of jewelry that might be for sale at a good price.

The search terms to type in the search bar are: Gold Chain, Gold Necklace, and Gold Bracelet.

Each search term will be searched for individually. For example: Search for Gold Chain. Then all the gold chains will pop up for sale in that area. Scroll through the whole page to see if you find a deal that meets your criteria.

Then repeat the same thing with the next search term which are then "Gold Necklace", and finally "gold bracelet."

I do one more search for "gold ring" but I do that search a bit different than the others. When I search for "gold rings" in the title, I always put a price range from 50-150 in the search bar. The reason I put the price range is because it filters out the ones with diamonds. Most gold rings aren't worth much, but if you find any 14k mens rings for

$100 or less they are usually ok to buy. They often won't know the weight of their rings, but if it looks a little thicker - $100 is a good price at today's price of gold. This pricing will obviously change with the gold price.

Finding the Deals

Follow the instructions from the CL search engine page to make sure your settings on CL are correct. Then start browsing using the search words and settings.

Occasionally, there will be ads with weights in penny weights (dwt) instead of grams. 1 DWT or pennyweight is 1.55 grams.

If they have a weight of their gold posted in the description, and they are asking somewhat close to what the value of the weight is make them an offer. For example, if the person is selling a 14k gold chain that is worth $400 to you and they are asking $450, offer them the $400 or $375 if you want room to barter with them.

The conversation would go as follows.

Email Subject: Gold Chain

Email Message: Hi I am wondering if you will accept $375 for your gold chain.

Thanks,

Chad

Then they will respond with either a yes, no, or a counter offer.

If they respond with no, you can either ignore it or you can reply with a short thanks for your time.

If they respond yes, ask them for their phone number and best time to reach them.

If they respond with a counter offer, look to see if the price is ok. On the initial offer, I often drop the price around 10% lower than what my final price would be just so you have room to work with if they give you a counter offer. Any counter offer that is above your price target just say thanks for your offer, but I will have to decline.

If the weight is not displayed, and it looks

like it might be a good deal, ask them the weight in the email. The email would go: Hi, do you by chance know the weight of your gold chain or whatever they are selling.

I usually always try to communicate with CL users by email first. The reason is because you can keep track of multiple discussions and deals without taking notes. When they reply to your email, there is a link to the item that you are discussing along with your entire log of communications. That way you don't have to keep track of everything for sale, and it is always in your records. You are going to be contacting anywhere from 5 to 20 people a week so either use the email system with your history of communication, or if you are good at keeping a log write down the communications you have had either by phone or email. Another thing you will want to do is copy and paste into your word program on your computer any deals that are outstanding and you want to make sure they are your top priority.

The reason why I try to find the weight prior is because you don't want to waste your time meeting people if you are questioning the deals. The more info you can find about the gold without meeting the person the better. Your time is valuable, and you shouldn't waste it by having to go out and weigh an item that is questionable. However, there are times when it makes sense to take the time to weigh an item yourself. As you get familiarized with the photos you will be able to determine the general weight of each item.

When you see something that your seller doesn't know the weight, but you think it looks like a good deal, go and weigh it yourself. Before you arrange a meeting with the person, tell them that you are looking to buy more gold, and ask them to bring any items they would like to sell. There have been times when I was going to purchase a small $100 bracelet, and when I called them to arrange a meeting I told them that I could buy any gold off them that they were looking to sell. The person ended up bringing a bunch of old gold they had laying around, and I walked out with $1,200 worth of gold. It seriously made both of our days. They were tremendously happy with the $1,200 and I was super happy to get a great deal on it!

I always like to give my customers a great price when they don't have a price in mind. I generally will not go 15% below spot price when buying gold from a customer that does not have an asking price. You want to give your customers good deals. If you give them a good price, they will be repeat customers and word of mouth will take off.

Sometimes I will bend this rule if they are asking a specific price, and I know it is a great deal. The reason is because they are already stating their price upfront, and if I give them what they are asking then it should make them pleased with their sale. For example, if they are asking $100 and I know it is worth $200, I will give them the $100 because that is what they are asking for.

You would be surprised on some of the deals you can find. One of my first purchases on Craigslist was for a ring that the person did not know the weight or karat (it wasn't stamped) but was asking $50. I actually met them and purchased the ring for $50 without weighing it. The very ugly ring was worth $300 in gold! Right then I realized that if you are patient, you can find some killer deals!

Below is my ugly ring deal. The ad said "Ugly Heavy Gold Ring For Sale"

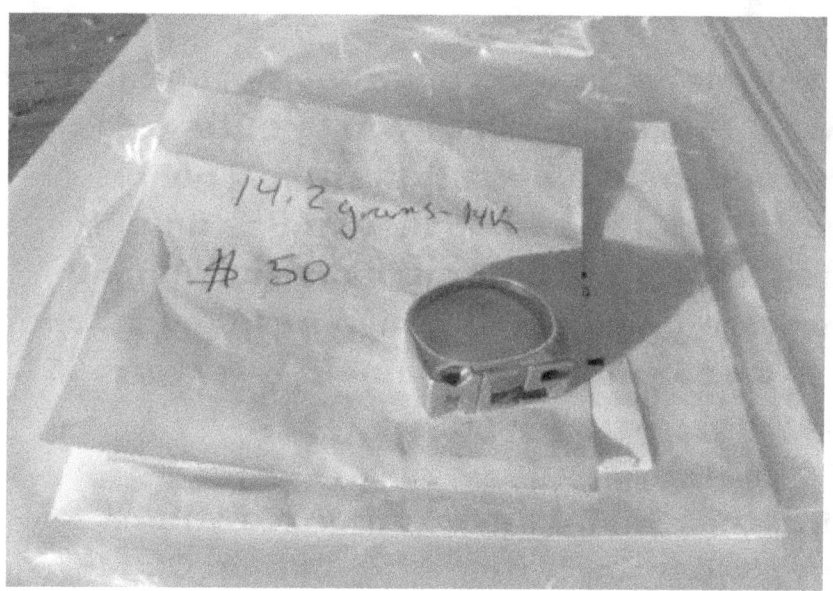

Don't Argue

Don't waste your time arguing with a craigslist user about the value of their gold.

Offer them a price below spot in their email or over the phone, and if they say no way just move on to the next deal. You can spend a little time bartering, but if you get the feel that the customer wants way more than what you want it for, don't offend the person with a rant about how their price is wrong.

If you make an offer and they decline it right away, it is an absolute waste of time to try and convince a person that their gold is worth less than what they are asking. If they have a pre determined price in mind, they are only going to cave in so much, and it is up to you to determine if it is worth it for you.

With that said, I have had cases where people had their items for sale on CL for over a month, and I offered them half their asking price which was 10% below spot, and they accepted because it was their best offer and they wanted to get rid of it.

As a general rule, I have found if you offer 25% below their list price, they often go with your offer. The longer they have their items for sale, the easier it is to talk them down in price.

Only make an offer that makes sense for you to buy. The worst case is they might laugh at you, but the key is to be respectful and not to argue with them about their price. Be polite, and if they don't accept your offer say thank you for your time and move on to the next deal.

Estate Sales

One of the best ways to purchase gold is at estate sales. I will warn you, it is very competitive and a bit intimidating, but often well worth it. You can often times find gold at these estate sales for half price.

Things to bring
A Snack
Calculator or phone calculator app
Proper Clothing
Gold Tester
Magnet
Scale

A secure bag
Cash
Check
Credit Card
GPS

The first thing you need to do is to find where the estate sales are at. I highly recommend using a website called www.estatesales.net. On there you can type in your location, and it will give you all the upcoming estate sales around your area. You then can click on each estate sale and look at the description and pictures of what they have for sale. This gives you an opportunity to see how much gold is potentially for sale at each location, and you can plan on going to the sales that you think are worth your time. Another nice feature on estatesales.net is that if you sign up with them, they will send you emails of the upcoming estate sales in your location.

You will find that often there are multiple sales per weekend. Study each one on your computer, and rank each sale from your top priority to low priority. Then map them all out and plan a strategic route that you think would be the most efficient as well as economical. It is probably best to go to your top sale first even if the location isn't in your routes favor. Starting off with great deals early in the day will allow you to make important decisions of how much more you want to buy after each deal you find - especially because the underpriced valuables usually sell very quickly.

Who knows, you might find so many deals at your first sale that you successfully complete your goals for that day, and you can go home.

Payment

Each estate sale is different. Some only accept cash. Some accept all forms of payment - credit cards, cash and checks. If you are unsure, look at the estate sale ad, or call the company hosting the sale. They will be able to tell you what forms of payment they accept. It is also important to note that every estate sale policy is different. Some charge a percentage processing fee and sales tax, so make sure you are aware of any fees that may arise before you start deciding what to buy. Each estate sale company should list the sales policy in their ad online.

Amateur Mistakes

The first estate sale I went to it was 10 below zero and after the house was full, they only let about 3 people in at a time. We ended up sitting outside in line for about 30 minutes before we got in, and we were freezing cold because we did not dress appropriately.

The second mistake I realized I made was looking for the gold first. I spent 5 minutes walking throughout the house looking for the gold before I asked. I found out the gold is in the most logical place which is right by the checkout so that the sellers can keep an eye on the valuables. Thinking back, it made so much sense where the valuables should be located, but being nervous and dodging a heard of people can sometimes affect your judgment. The lesson I learned was to make sure you have a plan where you think the gold is before you go in.

Time can sometimes be your enemy. When I finally found the gold for sale, I had a beautiful gold coin in my hand and was going to purchase it, but before I had time to check out, I was informed it was purchased just a minute before I decided to buy it! I then started weighing other items, and ended up buying a 14k ring for $100, and some silver for $50.

When I got back to my vehicle, I immediately looked at the ring. The lighting was dark inside the sale, and realized I more than likely purchased a ring that had no gold in it. It was tarnished, and gold does not tarnish. So I then tested it, and sure enough, there wasn't any gold in the ring I bought, and all sales are final. I was under pressure because it was literally like a black Friday sale where everyone is trying to grab stuff from you, and you don't have much time to make a decision. I didn't want to let the ring get away so I bought it without fully examining it. The lesson here is to make sure you take your time and examine the items for sale before you buy them.

If you have an electronic tester, make sure to bring it with you. Ask them if they guarantee the authenticity of the stamp, and if they don't guarantee it, then ask them if they would allow you to test it.

The next mistake I made was that I arrived there about 30 minutes late. Based on the description on the ad, I knew there was a lot more gold that was purchased before I got there. When I finally got through the line and into the house, most of the gold was gone. Even if I would have got there 5 minutes earlier, I would have walked out with that gold coin!

After making all these mistakes I was better prepared for my next estate sale adventure. I got there early, had a strategy to find the gold immediately, and was the first one in to start looking for the gold. I found several necklaces, and bracelets. I purchased the entire lot for $600 and the gold content was worth over $1,000. I did this all in one sale totaling about an hour. It was a success. By my second estate sale, I made up for the loss at my first sale and had a net profit.

Auctions

Auctions are a bit different than estate sales because you have to stay at the auction until the items come up that you want to bid on. This can be time consuming, but you can be rewarded for your time. In order to bid at a traditional auction, you must be comfortable to raise your hand and or voice in front of an audience to bid. This can be intimidating to some, but also exciting and fun to others. It kind of depends on your personality. I personally avoid public auctions.

If you don't like going to auctions, online auctions are a whole different ballgame. Online auctions allow you to bid for items at the comfort of your own home. Once you bid on an item, your competition has a chance to bid on that same item until the auction ends, and just like a traditional auction the person with the highest bid wins.

You can find online auctions near you by doing a google search. The website estatesales.net also has links to online auctions as well. They also provide information and photos of the items being sold at each auction.

It is important to read through the disclaimers of each auction you find. At most online auctions there is a fee that goes to the host. It is usually a percentage of the item you purchased. Also, there is a deadline date of when the item you purchase has to be removed from the auction. Shipping can also be arranged which can get expensive when you are purchasing valuable items.

Before you bid on any item in the auctions make sure you factor in any potential shipping, sales tax, and the processing fee. If you forget to subtract your expenses, you could end up with loss that you thought was originally a profit.

Garage Sales

The final place to look for gold is at Garage Sales. Garage sales can be a hit and miss. It is probably one of the most inefficient ways to buy gold, but if you have the patience, you can often find outstanding deals. Garage sales are like estate sales, but with even lower prices. Garage sales are often held by homeowners to get rid of clutter at an extremely attractive price. I've seen gold jewelry priced at garage sales for $25 that was worth over $100. The deals are outstanding, but the main problem is that not every garage sale has gold, and it is hard to know if they have gold for sale until you actually physically attend them. You can spend an 8 hour day going to garage sales to purchase $200 worth of gold. If you enjoy going to garage sales browsing other non gold items, this may be entertaining for you, but it really boils down to personal preference.

Recently, there has been "online garage sales" popping up everywhere on Facebook. These can be worth your time as you can browse the group every once in a while looking for deals at the convenience of your computer or smart phone.

Another advantage for Facebook garage sales is that you can post on the page that you are looking to buy gold jewelry, and people will comment and reply to your post.

You then can communicate with them on FB to see if the deal is worth it.

Keep in mind that you don't want to bombard these groups with posts constantly asking for gold jewelry. People might it find it annoying and complain. Keep it appropriate, and read the rules of the group so that you don't get kicked out.

Weekly Deals

One of the easiest and most efficient ways to find deals in your area is by signing up to my subscription based service – GoldPay Weekly Deals.

People often spend hours scouring through websites to find the sales or deals that are relevant around them. This service will save you a tremendous amount of time looking for the right places to go to.

We are constantly updating our gold searches in your area to relevant gold leads that could be a potential profit for you. Technology for gold searches is constantly changing, and we utilize it all to comb through your area for potential deals, and when we find them, we send you links to your inbox weekly.

Because the gold market is constantly changing, we often send gold market updates, and relevant tips to our subscribers so that they are in the loop.

This service is mostly for people that are going to make a career out of buying gold. However, I would encourage anyone that is reading this to sign up for a free one month trial even if you are purchasing in small amounts. After the free month, then you can decide if the information we send you is going to be valuable enough for a paid subscription. This is the only place you can get a free trial for this subscription so don't miss out on this $24.99 value for free! Find out more here: www.goldpay.us/deals

Storing Your Gold

After purchasing your items, you are going to want to keep them in a safe place. I recommend placing each item a zip lock sandwich bag. In the bag, I like to number the item with the date, weight, karat, and price paid. I then upload each item onto an excel spreadsheet so that I can keep track of my buys and sells and profit or losses.

After logging all the information, I then place the items in a combination safe for safe keeping. If you don't own a safe, it is not necessary to purchase one right away. It really is only necessary to buy a safe when you are storing several items for a period of time.

You can purchase safes for as little as thirty dollars to as high as several thousands of dollars.

Buying a safe depends on several factors:

- How much gold you plan on buying
- Your location

- How many people are in your household
- Who you are living with
- How well you trust your surroundings

It is going to have to be your judgment call of when to buy a safe and at what price you are willing to pay.

Selling your gold

After you find the deals, there are several different ways to sell your gold. Some of your items might be really unique, and you might want to try and sell it as a jewelry piece above spot price at first. It will take a lot longer for you to sell it, but it might be worth it for you. In general, I find that most jewelry for sale online is about double the spot price. So if the "melt value" of your gold item was $200 you could try and sell it for $400 as a jewelry piece.

When I buy something for a really good deal and consider it a unique enough piece of jewelry that someone might want to purchase it for a premium price, I have often used Craigslist and eBay as my vehicle for selling. The only setback to this approach is that you may not be able to sell it for the price you are asking, and you are risking the price of gold going down, and eventually selling it at break even or a loss. The gold price can fluctuate quite a lot from day to day month to month so it is important to be aware that if you decide to sell your item as jewelry, you could suffer a loss that was once a profit.

Posting your items on Craigslist, and eBay is simple to do. However, you are competing with a lot of sellers, and it is important to make your ad just right to stand out from the rest.

The first thing you need to do is clean the jewelry so that it shines in your photos. The next thing I recommend is to create a white background by a window with natural sunlight coming in. Place your jewelry on top of the white background and snap at least 10 photos with any kind of smart phone camera or professional camera. If you don't have a professional camera, a smart phone camera will do just fine as long as you get the lighting right.

You want to get several different camera views of your item for sale. Make sure you include a nice photo of the karat stamp to display in at least one of your photos.

The next thing you want to do is make your item stand out in the title and description. Use positive words like elegant, beautiful, stunning, rare, magnificent, etc. The words we choose to use are powerful. Choose them wisely.

Which ad title do you think would sell best out of the following two:

Ad Title #1: "For Sale Gold Necklace $600."

Ad Title #2: " Stunning Gold Necklace For Sale $600"

I am guessing you agree that Ad Title #2 is more attractive. One extra word in the title can make a big difference.

Once you have figured out your title. The description is the same thing. Choose your words wisely. Present your item with as much relative information that you can give without boring your customer. Include the weight, karat, length and width and any unique details that you can think of.

A good example would be

I have up for sale a stunning gold herringbone necklace. It is truly a one of a kind piece. This necklace looks brand new. It has been cleaned, and well taken care of.

Weight: 32 Grams
Metal: 14k Tested and Verified
Length: 18 inches
Width: 2.5 mm

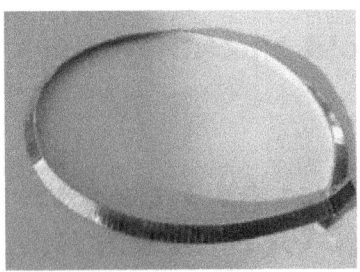

Once you come up with an ad, you can use the same description on both Craigslist and eBay. If you are selling on Craigslist you have to choose what form of communication you would like your buyers to use to get in touch with you. It is probably a good idea to allow them to get in contact with you through all forms of communication. That will make it easier to sell the item. After you receive an offer from someone, and are communicating by text or email, be sure to talk to them on the phone before you go and arrange a meeting with them. You can tell a lot from a person by hearing their voice.

I have had situations before where I was communicating with a buyer or seller through text or email, and when I finally arranged a meeting with them by phone call I immediately recognized that something was off, and I made an excuse and backed out of the deal. You have to use your judgment in these situations. When you find a deal through texting and you then call them and the conversation isn't flowing right, or that sixth sense is telling you that this doesn't seem right, listen to it. Make sure you have a backup plan when you run into these situations so that you know how to talk your way out of meeting someone if it doesn't feel right.

This is not to scare you away from buying and selling on Craigslist because 99% of the people are legit. I have done this a thousand times and have never once felt in danger, but it is important to be aware and smart about what you are doing. Always meet in a public place in a decent neighborhood. I would recommend meeting during the daylight at a coffee shop like Starbucks.

The last thing to note about CL is that a lot of people are going to waste your time with offers that are much lower than what you are asking. It really isn't that bad to just delete the offer or say no, but just to warn you it may be frustrating with how many offers you receive that are way below what you are asking.

Selling on Ebay

In order to sell on eBay you must have an account with eBay, and a PayPal account. They are very easy to set up, and once you have both you can start selling. Your eBay ad will look very similar to your Craigslist ad except there are a few different options available to enhance your sale. There are options to get your item to more people, photo number options, page enhancement, etc... all for a different uploading fee. You can also chose to either do a "buy it now" sale or an auction type sale.

Buy It Now Sale Vs Auction Sale

The "Buy It Now" feature is nice because it allows users to purchase your gold at any moment once it is up for sale. If you chose the auction feature it allows users to bid on your item for a certain period of time. You can set a starting bid which would be set at your lowest offer. From there it has the potential of being bid up to much higher levels than what you were originally asking for.

The setbacks of this feature is that sometimes people don't want to bid and will skip over your item to find a "buy it now" sale, and you also have to wait for a period of time for it to sell where the buy it now is an instant transaction.

The other setback is that you are responsible for shipping a very valuable item, and it is important that it is packaged and insured properly which can get expensive.

The final setback of eBay is that they have a listing fee and a selling fee, and both are a percentage based on the price of your item. These fees can get excessive because of how highly priced your items are. The fees also change from time to time. Check to make sure you have calculated all fees before you consider selling on eBay.

Selling Gold Fast

One of the problems you will run into is selling your gold fast at a decent price. The local pawn shops and gold shops seem to often be rip offs. The refineries pay a very fair price, but often have a minimum weight or other hidden fees. The other problem with sending your gold to a refiner is that you have to pay for the shipping, and insurance which can get expensive. Also, it can take over two weeks to receive payment depending on the refiner.

After realizing these setbacks, I decided to

open my own gold buying company called GoldPay www.goldpay.us. GoldPay is not another cheezy gold buying outfit. We offer revolutionary services with a great payout. If you know the weight and karat of your item, we will send you an instant prepayment before you ship your gold to us.

We not only prepay for your gold, but we also send you the labeled return package along with your payment. All you have to do after you cash your payment is follow the shipping instructions, and drop off your package at your local FedEx.

Also, if you don't have much money to start off and have some of your own gold that you don't wear anymore, you could utilize GoldPay to quickly turn your old gold into cash to jumpstart your gold buying career.

This is not a shameless plug. I stand behind my company, and believe we offer the best prices, and services out there. I truly want you to get the best potential profit you can make.

If you think you can get a better price for

your gold on eBay or Craigslist, by all means, go for it! Just keep in mind that GoldPay is a very safe, fair, and convenient option to sell your gold, and I stand behind it.

Conclusion

I hope by now you truly have a good grasp on what it takes to become a profitable gold buyer. By reading this book, you should have enough knowledge to go out and start buying whether it be with your own money or other people's money. As mentioned before, start with your friends and family, and move outward from there. As your confidence increases so will your ability to find deals.

I wish you the best of luck in your endeavors! I hope to be doing business with you someday with GoldPay. If you have any questions about our services, please feel free to contact us.

You can also email me directly at chadcastellanos@goldpay.us.

If you thought this book was helpful, I would appreciate your honest feedback by rating this book on Amazon.